This Book is given to you with only one request—
that you read it every day.

—from the *Gideon New Testament, Psalms and Proverbs*

FEAR NOT

Fear Not

MAURICE MIERAU

TURNSTONE PRESS

Fear Not
copyright © Maurice Mierau 2008

Turnstone Press
Artspace Building
018-100 Arthur Street
Winnipeg, MB
R3B 1H3 Canada
www.TurnstonePress.com

Turnstone Press gratefully acknowledges the assistance of the Canada Council for the Arts, the Manitoba Arts Council, the Government of Canada through the Book Publishing Industry Development Program, and the Government of Manitoba through the Department of Culture, Heritage, Tourism and Sport, Arts Branch, for our publishing activities.

Cover design: Jamis Paulson
Interior design: Sharon Caseburg
Printed and bound in Canada by Friesens for Turnstone Press.

Library and Archives Canada Cataloguing in Publication

Mierau, Maurice, 1962-

    Fear not / Maurice Mierau.

Poems.

ISBN 978-0-88801-338-5

    I. Title.

PS8576.I2858F42 2008   C811'.54   C2008-904555-6

For my father, a strong and skeptical reader of the Bible

CONTENTS

NEEDING PEACE ...

... the deepest problems are actually *not* problems.
—Ludwig Wittgenstein, *Tractatus* 4.003

FEAR NOT

TEMPTED TO COMMIT SUICIDE

1 How in Mel's snuff film Jesus groans in Aramaic.

2 And yet I feel nothing.

3 So let us crucify soft flesh on the cross in a musical comedy.

4 And the Soviets murdered my grandfather in 1938, before my father's memory begins. My grandfather did not try to run from the authorities, nor did he ride into Jerusalem on a donkey, waving a branch.

5 The earth did not shake nor did rocks split. My grandmother cut her finger on a knife. Her husband was nobody.

6 Let St. Paul himself claim to be nobody.

7 And let Ludwig say, "I conduct myself badly," thinking of the children he clouted on the side of the head when he taught them mathematics. A girl sprouted blood from her ear like a trick flower, and a boy fell unconscious.

8 So my father also is detached. And my heavenly father, he has nothing to do with the farcical cruelty below him.

9 And Judas went away and hanged himself.

10 But the man who betrayed my grandfather prayed and lived long.

11 So "enjoy your exotic moment responsibly."

ANXIOUS AND ...

Conscious of Sin

And he would have gladly filled his stomach with the pods that the swine were eating....

—Luke 15:16

1 *Now he said, "A man had two sons, and*

2 "on the younger son's bicep was a Chinese character whose meaning he probably misunderstood. The tattooed son said to his father, 'Give me the share of the estate that falls to me. Give it to me on a Visa prepaid card.' So his father divided his wealth between the sons on two such cards, and

3 "two days later, the younger son took an airplane to Cuba, and there he squandered his Visa card on sex tourism, every last pulsing decimal.

4 "After he had spent everything, he lived on the street,

5 "reciting bits of a Lorca poem he remembered from his desultory university career.

6 "Cubans sometimes gave him a few coins so he could eat, and the prostitutes gave him pomegranate seeds until the Canadian winter was over and the tourists went home.

7 "Maria, a young woman with an iPod, took pity on him,

8 "and he would have gladly stolen her iPod except that she had taken him home, taken and fed him, all as the rains began to fall,

9 "thousands of tunes nourishing him while he ate and realized that his father's lowliest employees were better off than he was—

10 *'early in the morning I will get up and go to my father, and say,* "Dad, I have done wrong to throw away your money from this Visa product, getting cash advances to

buy Bolivian marching powder and Colombian gold, assuming free trade works as it should on this utopian island that jails poets and homosexuals;

11 "retain me as a contract worker and do not call me your son anymore. I deserve no benefits or security,

12 "I beg you to text me with your decision."' "But his father's cell phone display was the colour of compassion, light blue as it hummed in the marble bathroom, and Daddy sent XOs to Maria's plain-Jane Nokia,

13 *"and the son said to him, 'Father, I have sinned against heaven and in your sight; I am no longer worthy to be called your son.'*

14 "'Listen,' said dad to his illegal immigrants, 'let's wire him money via a Canadian office of Western Union; and prepare the fresh sushi and goat when he arrives from the airport; for this son of mine has de-toxed on the seeds of a well-known anti-oxidant and my private jet's GPS flashes over Cuba.' *And lo, they began to celebrate though the goatless older brother was jealous."*

DISTRESSED OR TROUBLED

[for Harry Lehotsky, Winnipeg inner city activist and Baptist minister, 1957–2006]

1 The cancer looks bad but God makes it good,

2 hence *good God* is a way to say horror.

3 The Reverend Lehotsky knows he is dead,

4 he already knows my predestined sorrow—

5 hence *good God* is a way to say horror.

6 But now in July neither's said, no one is sad:

7 he already knows my predestined sorrow,

8 for the reverend's justified and glorified.

9 But now in July what is said

10 is goodbye to my friend whose body I touch,

11 for the reverend's justified and glorified,

12 convinced that neither death nor much

13 can be a real goodbye to those he will touch.

14 This Sunday he is a sheep to the cancer,

15 convinced that neither death nor much

16 can stop him seeing the contractor upstairs, and dancing.

17 This Sunday he is a sheep to the cancer—

18 the cancer looks bad but God makes it good.

19 Can it stop him seeing the contractor upstairs?

20 The Reverend Lehotsky knows he is dead.

FRIENDS FAIL

[for the contestants on *America's Next Top Model*, season three, originally broadcast in fall 2004]

But the Lord stood with me and strengthened me, so that through me the proclamation might be fully accomplished, and that all the Gentiles might hear.

—2 Timothy 4:17

1 Concrete splits, eyeliner runs,
project software

2 crashes. You must forgive your
failing friends

3 but only if they repent.
They repent by staying thin and
swallowing the product.[1]

4 They repeat up to seven takes.
Maximum.

5 I myself am covered in tarantula,[2]
the stare

6 of Janice, twitching fake-boobed
judge,[3] the lens

7 trained on the product

8 blows bodies from the room,
bums

9 out of seats. You don't care,

10 you're from Oklahoma where
strong men

11 smell and fathers fail. They
forsake you if rents

12 rise, if the medicine cabinet
lacks Tums,

13 but why should you care, the
Lord made you Cassie of the bare[4]

14 proclamation to the Gentiles.

15 So your adversaries' desire
dents

---

1 Several contestants had difficulty swallowing the Japanese food product during an advertising shoot in episode 9 of *ANTM*, fall 2004.

2 Contestants had to pose with tarantulas on their faces for a photo shoot in episode 8.

3 Former model Janice Dickinson was one of the judges.

---

4 Cassie was an Oklahoma-based exotic dancer before appearing on the show.

16 your heart. False witnesses
breathe rotting crumbs,

17 even your close friend in whom
you confide, she dares

18 lift her Prada high heel pumps
in scorn

19 over you. How can you get
revenge?

20 Your enemy joyous but Tyra[5]
makes her numb

21 unlike Yaya[6] the Ivy League
bitch, who blares

22 that plans fail and friends fail
and yes Stonehenge

23 fell, partly. And yet, your folly,
you shall love your dumb

24 failing friends with all your
failing, falling tears.

---

5 Tyra Banks, former supermodel, host and
producer of the show.

6 Camara "Yaya" Da Costa was the runner-up
for this season.

ILL OR IN PAIN

Therefore I am well content with weaknesses, with insults, with distresses, with persecutions, with difficulties, for Christ's sake; for when I am weak, then I am strong. —2 Corinthians 12:10

1 Some mystical power emanates from me that will yet be bolstered by the state.

2 Brag about your weakness!

3 Don't make me threaten you.

4 The elders of the church will pour oil on the sick—but not hot, to avoid injury or awakening of the darkness.

5 How the sick will be cured and also forgiven if they have done anything wrong. This covers, for example, shady real estate transactions and hate crimes.

6 Your youth renews like an eagle's. A good simile, but the habitat's vanishing, really a mess.

7 The high voltage of Christ flows through me, capable of causing serious injury to me or to you. Once warned you can't sue.

8 It's perfect to be powerless,

9 call me names, call me helpless, call me crazy, harvest my organs while I lie awake.

10 When my flesh rots because you are angry, my bone marrow extracted to a G-8 country,

11 oh what it would cost to rob the light of my eyes, to do

12 it legally, Lord you make me confess,

13 oh what it would cost to rob the light of my eyes

14 when my flesh rots because you are angry, my bone marrow extracted to a G-8 country for less.

15 Harvest my organs while I lie awake, call me helpless, call me crazy, call me names,

16 it's powerless to be perfect.

17 Once warned you can't sue, not me and not you. The high voltage of Christ flows through me, capable of causing serious injury.

18 A good simile, but the resource is vanishing, really a mess. Your youth renews like an eagle's.

19 This covers, for example, shady real estate transactions and hate crimes. Also how the sick will be cured and forgiven if they have done anything wrong.

20 The elders of the church will pour oil on them—but not hot, to avoid injury or awakening of the darkness.

21 Don't make me threaten you.

22 Brag about your weakness!

23 Some mystical power emanates from me that will yet be bolstered by the state.

BEREAVED / BROKENHEARTED

... and He will wipe away every tear from their eyes; and there will no longer be any death; there will no longer be any mourning, or crying, or pain; the first things have passed away.
—Revelation 21:4

1 You must know about those who brush their teeth and fall asleep uninformed.

2 Without high speed Internet, they are bereaved and brokenhearted, grieving and asleep.

3 How Jesus was reborn:

4 Not like this. They hold him and fall asleep.

5 But for you who fall asleep in front of a screen, the right way,

6 drinking words like blood on the floor of an interrogator's cell,

7 you'll get there before those with electric toothbrushes, on that day,

8 shouting like a soccer fan the Lord descends, his voice trumpet-pure, and the Christly dead arise.

9 We who remain breathing, in the blink of a power surge, we meet the cirrus clouds and the Lord's eyes

10 inside the tooth-whitener find a booming woofer, God's A/V device saying to you, tainted toothpaste may contain

11 diethylene glycol, forever toxic, an inexpensive sweetener and thickening agent, commonly found in solvents and antifreeze.

12 Death will not retain its first sting, its pain that passes all.

13 In the end no one buys dollar store toothpaste anyway.

JUST RETIRED

After Matthew 6:33, 34

1 Looking for his kingdom, you
must get along at night, no
inflation allowance or new

2 income source, your bony leg
light like an old chicken or hair
sprouting decayed string—

3 it's the kingdom of cheap horror
where the unanswered telephone
and the personal care home's door

4 open like flesh rejects bone, each
of us stuck with the other waking
uncaffeinated at dawn,

5 each day has enough bother so
long after saying I do, I do, cleaving
unto job or you, not my mother.

6 All these things added through
someone who's true—maybe you.
Maybe you.

IN DANGER OR THREATENED

And there arose a fierce gale of wind, and the waves were breaking over the boat so much that the boat was already filling up.

—Mark 4:37

1 And they said my grandfather sang religious words with his youth choir, and poisoned pigs on the animal farm. His accuser was another God-ridden man.

2 And my grandfather would not stop singing Jesus, Jesus, Jesus. We don't know what his number was in prison, but it was up.

3 And he would not stop, not run, not sign the confession. He practically shot himself.

4 And courage is rational as long as you float.

5 He sank.

6 He sank with the bullet in his head on February 2nd, 1938.

7 *And the wind died down and it became perfectly calm.*

NEEDING . . .

ADVICE ON BEING A MAN

[for my son Jeremy at seventeen]

1 Never use the fly in your boxers. If there are exceptions don't remember them.

2 Remember that a nuthatch is smarter than the poplar tree it clings to.

3 Always shoulder check. Blind spots are real, change is real, and metal sluices through flesh.

4 Never call back for clarification except if you change your mind. Change your mind like a cat, completely and quickly.

5 Remember if you have to cry in front of a woman or someone you love, especially a man, save it up and then pour it out like a collapsing sea wall, let yourself choke on the salt, leave the stains on your face like an alkali pit or a deserted dock. Cry silently.

6 Remember that the crow in the tree watches the cat.

7 Never be the crow.

8 Remember seeing your first lover getting out of bed and how the light plays over you both.

9 Always stare at the moon after you have sex.

10 Never wear a polka-dotted tie.

11 Remember I love you and I may not speak every word of this out loud.

12 Always call home on Sundays. I will wait for your call.

ADVICE ON BEING A LEADER

1 Success is a choice that helps you discover the leader within and your Ray Type. Now we will teach you to apply your knowledge of the Seven Energies active in the world today.

2 Not everyone can be a leader.

3 On the Naked News website on September 11, 2001, there were seven men and women who read the news while calmly, not erotically, taking off their clothes. Their motions were a bit jerky on the live video feed, much like the collapse of the towers on TV.

4 Often a leader benefits by not letting others know what he's up to. (That's why chemotherapy is like the invasion of a foreign country; the cancer does not know what is to come, no, nor where it is going.)

5 I know four things about you that no one else does.

2 Did you ever wonder why so much is composed of seven major energies? Seven colours in the rainbow, seven musical notes, seven types of human personality and soul.

2 There is no more powerful motivation for others than a leader who sets an example. (Deposits in a Swiss bank account are not part of the example.)

3 That's why the Siege of Stalingrad is an important model. Those who refused to fight were lined up and shot.

4 Sports, business and life are one. I love you, you are not a model, these are just ways of speaking.

3 Multi-Level Marketing (MLM) is not the same as a pyramid scheme. Everyone needs vitamins and jewelry.

2 Discover your own Ray Type to understand your strengths and weaknesses. Find your life purpose and career within the Seven Ray Fields.

3 Leaders foster alignment at all times. Alignment does not mean everyone shoots at the same time without following protocol.

4 Second source everything, including natural resources. Remember what happened to Hitler.

5 Your shape too is beautiful.

4 One of a leader's responsibilities is to meet the needs of those he or she leads. Needs and wants cannot be successfully differentiated.

(Many women feel safer and more powerful riding up high. Men like to purchase chrome-plated grille guards for their SUVs.)

2 Understand the Seven Basic Energies of the universe and how you can be more effective by working with them to manage human capital.

3 Let Pat Riley help you find the winner within. Have you lost money today?

4 Leadership means science and profit walk hand in hand. I love how you walk.

5 Not all our allies wash their hands, though some do.

6 It is time to merge and end this talk of love.

ADVICE ON BEING A PRO ATHLETE

Our little systems have their day
  They have their day and cease to be....
—Alfred Lord Tennyson, Prologue to "In Memoriam"

1 Sacrifice your body, that's the spirit,

2 worship the Escalade purchased with your

3 rookie contract. Don't conform to this world,

4 just provide the sample, don't fear it,

5 don't be a mule or a baton twirled

6 out of a girl's hand and into the sun;

7 bit, bridle or gravity stop the soar

8 of little systems, cheerleaders back-lit

9 in the shine of CO_2-spewing Love, God's one

10 Caucasian face whom we by arena light

11 well, embrace.

THANKFULNESS

1 To the apartment complex in its ugly simplicity, paint scabbing off the balcony pilings

2 To the bullet holes in buildings just like this one, in foreign countries

3 To the shining hubcaps of this car

4 To feeling tired and hopeful

5 To moving your car quickly when the man comes to give you a ticket

6 To learning how your body flows through rooms when I'm not there

7 To the digital recording of everything I am going to tell you

8 To knowing nothing and understanding a little

9 To clarity of feeling

10 To knowing how the story ends

11 To this shirt scented innocent from the laundry

12 To the elegance of a smashed car window

13 To the deer in the yard perfect as a computer animation

14 To the man on the cherry picker replacing light bulbs

15 To the woman with sunglasses and cigarette

16 To the spit you spat on the sidewalk

17 To the keys bunched on your belt

18 To the silver cars

19 To my father for always being right

20 To the clarity of your grammar and the line of your legs

21 To the drunk who stopped to ask for something

AFRAID

Jesus was in the stern, asleep on the cushion; and they woke him and said, "Teacher, do you not care that we are perishing?"

—Mark 4:38

1 Jesus stood up in the crooked boat. He told wind and waves to shut up.

2 Jesus said fire-walking with Tony Robbins works the same way.

3 Those who remember fill with light, and those who forget have rotten fillings.

4 And if you discover a dead body you know the world like Philip Marlowe and vice versa.

5 After the storm you still have "5,000 songs in your hand." The iPod is not advised for soldiers.

6 After the war Ludwig spoke about "misunderstandings concerning the use of words."

7 *And He said to them, "Why are you afraid?"*

CONSIDERING...

MARRIAGE

1 How in the flesh of two one prevails.

2 Yet the wife headless without her man, the man all giant head and bodyless, emheaded and red, bloodless and strange, cocky and encrusted in words.

3 Or the man with two heads, one talking to the headless mouthless wife, the other screaming at her disconnected body.

4 And "miserable is the body that depends on another body."

5 Or the two are one flesh, wrinkleless like the washing of water.

6 And "remember you're watering yourself with filtered water that your body truly appreciates."

7 Or by loving yourself you love your wife. Conjoined twins, you do not even need to speak.

8 Wordlessly you reach across each other's thighs.

9 Your brains share the same lining, and surgeons shake their heads.

DIVORCE

1 Moses allowed a man to write a certificate of divorce and send her away.

2 But "I am aware of the complete unclarity of all these sentences," wrote Ludwig, who read every story in *Detective Story Magazine*, even the ones about divorce.

3 And "nothing sucks like an Electrolux."

4 How that was the problem.

5 Whoever divorces and marries again commits adultery.

6 Whoever commits adultery is male or female, half of an inseparable God-made double now rent apart and then united with someone else, driven by biology, love, money, whimsical desire, permanent lust, or all the smells of this world.

7 And what I feel when I see you walking down the hall in your panties.

Sexual Immorality

1 How Mary was a nice girl. So was Sue. Either way he had to make a commitment, it said so somewhere.

2 It was a hot day with its own ambitions.

3 Perhaps reading about the war would help him.

4 Perhaps the hot day would unfold in some way that meant something.

5 But where would he read about his father, or Mary, or Sue?

6 The newspaper said someone with Sue's sign was too emotional, too sensitive, and extremely good at getting away with things.

7 His father had offered to lend him money.

8 His horoscope said if a friend offers you something, turn it down.

9 But was his father *a friend*? Should he choose Mary or Sue?

10 The cat moved and its bell rang.

11 And the swallows on the cornice scattered in the air like shrapnel.

DOUBT

1 Jesus spat on the blind man's eyes—actually he spat on his bland pale hands first, then he rubbed the man's eyeballs and the man saw how pale people look like trees, moving.

2 And the people stopped looking like moving trees, and the sea levels rose. Anything is possible etc.

3 And the officer was willing to believe anything, another great example.

4 "Enjoy your exotic moment responsibly," he said.

5 Jesus would have talked to Katrina, quietly. Anything is possible.

6 To doubt, Ludwig said, you must spend many years not doubting.

DEATH

1 Jesus was tempted on the cross but he remained perfect in his skimpy underwear.

2 "The next best thing to naked!"

3 But "intimate apparel is not exchangeable due to its intimate nature."

4 Mary in her skimpy underwear was Barbarella, a blonde angel having sex with the moon.

5 But is that true of Mary, or my grandmother?

6 How she married a second man who also failed to rise from the dead and protect her. Neither was blond.

7 Jesus lives, as Elvis did, in a house with many rooms.

8 And you won't be stuck sharing those rooms.

9 How like a giant Kleenex, God comes down and wipes all moisture from your face.

Inadequacy

1 I am the soldier shooting in the dark without night vision goggles. I have a problem with clutter.

2 And building new storage space transforms character on the Learning Channel.

3 Helen was my grandmother's name and also the face that launched etc.

4 Anything is possible for the rich.

5 And it is possible to say anything.

6 How they raped my grandmother in 1945 because of her language, because of their language, because the German estate was so beautiful.

7 But I am weak from forming these words, inadequate to change anything, to be ready.

8 And the limits of language are, Ludwig wanted to say.

9 The limits.

10 How you can be spiritual and have nice things.

BITTER OR CRITICAL

1 Take your finger out of your brother's eye and stop gouging at the speck you imagine itching there.

2 Ludwig said, "You are placed in the world like your eye in its field of vision." Jesus spoke the same way.

3 But in twilight, the loss of night vision from laser surgery affects the sleepless with their rotten fillings.

4 Take a dreamless sleep. Do not dream of dropping pearls in front of hogs on an industrial farm. They could trample you as you reach down to recover your memory, verse by verse.

5 My father says he does not remember when his mother was gang-raped by Russian soldiers.

6 How "Nothings sucks like an Electrolux." But that's just the obstacle of words.

7 Take my father. Where was he? Was he afraid?

8 Wake early in the morning and search for what you've lost. The surgeon left a tiny flap of skin in your eye. You find it with the rats, lying by the road.

TROUBLED BY LANGUAGE AND . . .

FAILURE COMES

1 How the flesh fails. And the heart fails also, as do the pipelines, sinking.

2 And like Tony Soprano at his barbeque God hands out portions for everyone, even the most despised.

3 I was disturbed, sleepless. Your eyes so big when I left your mother the trees pitched forward as if a storm blew.

4 No storm blew.

5 How drunk the spruce trees at right angles in the ditch.

6 And the trees were just a metaphor, a failure.

7 I need "the makeup of makeup artists."

8 Nothing I say could make you forgive me.

1 We love you and want you to owe us money. We want you to drink, drink, but not be drunk or otherwise irresponsible or unable to pay. It is our wish for you to live in the corporeally embodied moment, to slather self-tanning lotion all over if that is indeed appropriate for your skin tone, and to say

2 YES YES loudly as you allow your card to be scanned by any one of the millions of merchants equipped to do so. If you want flowers, cars, incense-free non-carcinogenic candles, discreet escort services, children's toys, home theatres, or cash advances that leave no e-trail, all of these are part of this bliss we ask you to join.

3 You may wish to purchase a speeding up of your body's functions, if that to you is bliss, or you may want to slow down; all of these wishes are legitimate and can be charged.

4 There is a reality principled minimum monthly balance of course but that is not what anyone needs to think of right now.

5 In fact we are very concerned that you have not used the PIN number we gave upon issue of this card for cash advances. We have kept track. We list it for your information at the top right. When you have read and memorized this number, eat a large meal at a restaurant that takes our card, and with your entrée chew the upper part of this letter into a rich paste. Spit it in water and be sure to flush it yourself in the nearest washroom.

6 Some things should not be left to the busboy.

7 Now break free! Perhaps there are beauty products you require. Is there music that will help you work? Pleasure is not a principle but a fundamental thing, something we can all truly grasp but only.

8 Success is guaranteed only if you go forth. Be in all things determined, charging, charged. Above all be going forth. Charge now! As you use our product, none of what happens is that dramatic: ones and zeros change places, and in some precisely calculated time never quite thirty days, we will speak to you again, and again.

1 In Nigeria a local rapper tried stealing the first class seats on a chartered jet belonging to 50 Cent and his posse.

2 I saw a beer bottle on a street's furrowed snow, brown and obscene, reflecting Christmas lights.
Her round-shaped ipaq looks around however a given white soft frog got an idea.

3 A Winnipeg architect pleaded guilty to child porn possession. He said it was difficult to spend time alone.

4 The salmon-farming company says that GM salmon are like more fuel-efficient cars.
Our hairy odd-shaped mobile phone adheres. A well-crafted recycle bin scowls.

5 At Buckingham Palace, a man dressed as Batman climbed onto a balcony to demand more rights for divorced fathers. He will face no charges.

6 Desire wraps itself in stained freezer paper, in holding back, in tongues intertwined and spines aligned, in the low bandwidth of the telephone's murmur.
His soft round car runs. The children's boat shows its value.

7 In Canada someone smashed the window on our car and took the stereo, the power amp, the subwoofer from the trunk.

8 In China a thousand farmers lost their land, without compensation, so a highway could be built.
Her silver baby smiles at the place that our tall house stinks.

Faith is Weak

1 How much more valuable than birds are you!

2 Certainly we would not risk capital on birds, nor on lilies.

3 As for our father, he was a minority shareholder.

4 When it comes to the conviction of things not seen, suspend *habeas corpus.*

5 Through faith we speak stronger than the smell of a corpse at a hundred metres.

6 Even after death we speak with certainty and conviction of our right to believe in Peter over Thomas, Abel over Cain, in Noah over everybody not on the boat.

7 God wanted a pair of clean animals or maybe seven pairs. The sons of Noah scrubbed the animals with an all-purpose household cleanser.

8 The flood lasted 40 days or 150, depending what we mean by *flood.* And the children of Noah violated the rainbow's contract.

9 God needed the rainbow like a Post-it note in the sky to remind him to keep the heavenly taps turned off.

10 The dove came back with a fresh olive leaf and dropped it like a feather in Noah's hand. And the dove spoke again after the flood, which made God less absent-minded.

Sleepless

1 How God has caused the wicked to need a lot of dental work.

2 And made teeth shatter into little white flecks as they fly like disease polyps!

3 And you can dream with "5,000 songs in your hand."

4 But I am not afraid of 10,000 soldiers surrounding me.

5 So please say something while you're holed up in your holy mountain.

6 How that would help me sleep.

7 And you can dream.

8 And everyone needs a second car, a second refrigerator, an alternate payment method.

9 But it takes four different emotions in succession to create a complete release.

10 So that's a bit eastern but it might help you.

ALONE

1 Mother dead, father gone—also
dead—and three languages in
as many years, not counting the
language of land mines, tanks, black
smoke, then more intimate speech:

2 Shovel for grave, orange and
sugar for luxury, lipstick for free,
come here for rape, field for beets,
ditch for grave.

3 Howling alone by a river where
no one heard him, my father
orphaned at ten in Germany, in
1947, already a linguist, ventriloquist
too, his sister heard him throwing
his voice, watched it walk across
water where every few steps it
hardened into the voice that later
talked through a violin, or painted
bony trees beside naked Canadian
lakes, walked out of three careers
filled with moral outrage, loved
watching sports on TV, never spoke
Russian after his mother told him
not to, never spoke in anger or
confusion that filled him in the early
spring day, on a river in Germany,
losing the language of children.

TEMPTED TO LIE

1 As my grandfather lies on the ground, knowing completely the bullet in his neck, the exit wound bleeds away.

2 He sacrifices his body as a career choice. Why does he not lie to save himself? Because he counts on the end of winter, a new body and a new earth.

3 As there are many members in an army or a church, each has its own identical function, some as Viagra, others false unicorn root, Levitra, or Cialis.

4 "Will you be ready?" say the soldiers.

5 When the Germans invade in 1941 there are still some bad apples around.

6 But bless those who curse you, even though it won't make any difference. And vice versa.

7 In 1943 fifty people march down the village road, wordless.

8 As the soldiers shoot them at the lip of a ditch, every last Jew in town, the winter coats in every size lie empty by the ditch, wordless and afraid.

9 My father is four years old. He will remember nothing before those people lying in the ditch. Like God and Ludwig and his father before him, my father speaks German. He sees those bodies march down the dirty Slavic road.

10 They cry without sound.

ANGRY AND ...

Insulted or Intimidated

After David's morning prayer in Psalm 3

1 Bless the blue house where you
live.
Bless the red suffering river

2 that flows with no lies in her
mouth,
whose high waters deliver

3 shattered teeth to my enemies
looking for dentures in the trees.

4 Selah I know means pause,
interlude or crescendo. Attitude

5 is all, positive attracts positive,
there's nothing rude

6 about wanting cash and power if
you're patient like a rower

7 who blesses the stormy moon,
who sleeps while Diana Krall
croons,

8 who yells at the holy mountain.
You yelled for an entire month,

9 cursing the blue house where
you live,
God-words drowned in the river.

Contemplating Revenge

1 How I fantasize about going to a high school reunion in a stretch-customized Hummer.

2 I arrive at high speed, and get out languorously, with a woman as trophy on my elbow.

3 She is Asia Argento, pornographically beautiful and with tattoos in painful places, speaking slowly in long sentences with swollen-lipped words.

4 I got rich in the electronics industry, having begun with a mail-order electrical engineering degree and then conquering through sheer brilliance, force of personality and size of penis.

5 My manufacturing plant was in the small town where I attended high school. The plant was made out of industrial steel like a granary, and inside I employed, at miserable child-labour wages, all the half-wits who went to school with me.

6 Every few years, on my orders, the foreman set a fire in part of the plant after locking the exits, killing one or two workers randomly, and then let the rest out at the last minute. They choked, spittle dotting their middle-aged multiple chins, their perpetually '70s hair burnt so they looked like chemo patients.

7 Sometimes after the fire the foreman shot the least productive ones into ditches that they dug themselves.

8 The foreman was my best employee.

Contemplating Revenge (once more)

1 My girlfriend kept grabbing at my crotch salaciously and we entered the gym. I gave a speech on leadership to the graduating class of my alma mater.

2 I wore an Italian suit and a cambric shirt with a bowtie made out of leather and dead bats' wings. I had just spent more than Martin Amis on perfecting my teeth.

3 My bodyguard took Ron, an old nemesis of mine, outside during the speech. Beat him with a short rubber pipe like the Russian secret police, leaving no marks.

4 All my favourite teachers were in the front row, out of retirement or back from the dead, beaming at me. Mrs. Von Adel, my English teacher, coloured her hair blonde instead of her usual orange. When Ron came back in from getting the shit kicked out of him, Mrs. V hit him slam in the kidney with a Complete Shakespeare.

5 "Ooohf," he said.

6 Ron's wife was still pretty in an in-bred sort of way. At the exit she asked if she could join Asia and me for a threesome. I agreed.

7 And she wept as if I'd said no.

Desperate (at your wits' end)

1 I whine and complain and you have a lot of time for that, which is great oh God.

2 Your wings are like a superhero's cape, flaring, a refuge from the enemies these pills do not erase.

3 You are a great tower, a tent, an engorged Lincoln Navigator with transparent condom. Selah.

4 The man and the woman each in their own bathtub, as the voice speaks softly, "Will you be ready?"

5 And my enemies perform extraordinary rendition on me to extract a confession. They know that bathtubs are not always bathtubs, nor are any objects familiar or innocent:

not walls
not windows
not doors
not refrigerators
not chairs
not beds

6 How I lift my eyes to the hairless extremities of pornography and askjolene.com for "On Her Knees," "BBW," "Snowball," "Gagging," "Goo."

7 The pain from which confession springs is always true.

8 And the object of war is to increase suffering.

Looking for a Job / Made Redundant

1 The outplacement counseling
and severance,

2 the letter to sign, Christ's voice
in your head, your guide,

3 and the box with your personal
effects,

4 the walk to the elevator outside

5 the corporation's fortress.

6 Speak a prayer for deliverance
from grey cubicles and the stale air
you envy and long for. What's

7 next?

8 The personality test shows you
cannot extrovert just to impress.

9 Once

10 the graphs print out in dark red
and black—

11 they won't take you back. Your
back is the face of an introvert. And
so is your face.

12 You have been put out. Your
e-mail account deleted. Your door
fob deactivated.

VICTIMIZED

But the humble will inherit the land
And will delight themselves in abundant prosperity.
—Psalm 37:11

1 The wicked are insecure and they drive in high vehicles. Selah.

2 Do not fret for it leads to evildoing, and evildoers will be cut off, yea, starting with their lower limbs.

3 Or they'll be vaporized by an IED so fast their blood burns before hitting the ground. Do not fret.

4 You are up high, in the airplane looking down. See the dogs feast on your enemies. Their children look innocent now and soon they will be corrupted ah hah.

5 They do not understand. Not everyone can have a tanning bed for all his limbs.

6 The wicked are insecure and they drive in high vehicles. Selah.

7 The pawn shop sells swords and cell phones with tones fa la.

8 In church they sing hymns.

9 But still they will be vaporized by an IED so fast their blood fries before hitting the ground. Do not fret.

10 On our blood-infected land falls manna.

11 When our enemies appear they are desert holograms.

12 The wicked are insecure and they drive in high vehicles. Selah.

13 Like an aging '80s rock star spraying Jack Daniel's from his groin onto the heads of pretty kneeling soccer moms, voom va va.

14 Let not your arteries harden. Nor our children watch while the screen dims.

15 Or they'll be vaporized by an IED so fast their blood fries before hitting the ground. But not yet. Do not fret.

16 Just walk to the next letter like Vanna.

17 Your organic fair trade dark roast coffee brims, as with happiness you brim.

18 You are up high, in the airplane looking down. See the dogs feast on your enemies, see their entrails out of focus on the video. Their children look innocent now and soon they will be corrupted ah hah.

19 You yourself will be vaporized poof by an IED so fast your blood roasts well before hell's gate. But do not fret. Not yet.

LONELY

The Tao enables the male member to become an all-weather instrument of equal competence to that of its female counterpart ... while at the same time protecting the health and prolonging the lives of both partners.

—from Daniel Reid, *The Tao of Health, Sex and Longevity,*
<http://www.hps-online.com/tsy4.htm>

1 Taoists say too much ejaculating makes a man prematurely senile or vulnerable to disease by robbing him of his primary source of vitality and immunity.

2 Twenty percent of male semen is composed of cerebrospinal fluid, and the loss of zinc in ejaculate makes a man vulnerable to Alzheimer's (madness) and hypersensitive to sunlight (blindness); it stands to reason that men should not have sex at all or only by Taoist principles (no masturbation):

3 *only come twice a month.*

TEMPTED TO COMMIT SEXUAL IMMORALITY (AGAIN)

And besides you, I desire nothing on earth.
—Psalm 73:25

1 How the body's a dirty book lying on the bed right there.

2 But the Lord is for the body and vice versa. Food is for the stomach, but both will decompose when God finds a way.

3 And composting solves most ethical problems, you have to admit.

4 You know Jesus fed the five thousand, and the disciples took those twelve leftover baskets and traded them for sexual favours and Bible verses.

5 But witness the fate of homosexuals, the gnashes and wailings of, upon whose heads walls fall because they live among us or the terrorists.

6 "You are unable to notice something—because it is always before your eyes," said Ludwig, who wanted to marry a woman, at least in words.

7 But I feel happiness when I see you in your panties, walking down the hall.

8 How outside your home the crew of pervertedjustice.com waits to put you on TV. You are eager. You are afraid. You're afraid, aren't you?

FURTHER TEMPTED BY ...

DRINK ABUSE

And do not get drunk with wine, for that is dissipation, but be filled with the Spirit....

—Ephesians 5:18

1 Drunks get drunk at night,
except in daylight

2 when they also drink. Then the
sober love

3 to watch trees bending visibly in
the wind like spruce

4 do in melting permafrost, and
they see

5 a tree bending drunk, human as a
twelve-step pamphlet in the wind.

6 The drunks know the trees are
not just trees, trite figures,

7 but sleepwalkers in the lean
night,

8 amnesiacs drinking, driving in
the invisible dark.

9 The sober say let the stumbling
light make dissipation visible

10 so all we see is light—

11 spirited with piss and God's
glory—

12 Wake up! Be sober as your LED
nightlight,

13 lower the missile defense shield
you call love

14 and freeze the melting
permafrost of hope.

DRUG ABUSE

a love Psalm

1 With your hands weaving me *in utero*

2 knowing my thin arm tracks, intimate,

3 knowingly you enclose me *ex nihilo,*

4 this accident of the wordy palate

5 makes also accidental the design meme,

6 the lady drying tea stains in a

7 microwave and fortune telling nothing

8 since the body's after all a temple

9 where no rat presides like Jesus or Sun Ra,

10 on the make and on the seam

11 between legal knowledge that knows nothing

12 and my desire to sing:

13 the flap of electronic nerve endings

14 humming like a cat.

PRAYING / READING GRAFITTI

One of His disciples said to Him, "Lord teach us to pray just as John also taught his disciples."

—Luke 11:1

1 Lost among the tags and wrinkled safes, *I left my heart under the Maryland Bridge.*

2 *Our father.* He is locked in there with the children.

3 *I'm looking for some head Leave #*

4 On the side of his body there is a ridge.

5 Seek, and you will find another path to the river. How many have fallen here, all these chilled men?

6 *I left my heart under the Maryland Bridge.*

7 ♥ *Ruth punk as* fff-idgets.

8 Asked for an egg, do you get a scorpion?

9 *for some head Leave #*

10 *Give us each day our daily Gidget.*

11 And forgive us our area clearance.

12 *I left my heart under the Maryland Bridge.*

13 If hallowed be your excessive rigidity

14 you might get snakes for every ten fishes.

15 *for some Leave #*

16 And lead us not into daddy's fridge.

17 ♥ *Ruth punk as* fidgets.

18 *I left my heart under the Bridge.*

19 *some #*

FEAR

And He said to them, "Why are you afraid? How is it that you have no faith?"
—Mark 4:40

1 Jesus stood up in the crooked air. He told wind and waves. Shut up, he said, just like Neptune had on some other ocean.

2 Ludwig and Jesus both spoke English.

3 There are many words in English, and each word has its own function.

4 After Jesus fed the five thousand the disciples wrote Bible verses with ballpoint pens on the people's hands.

5 And Ludwig said to them, "I am afraid." But the problem was he had only his own language in which to say he was afraid.

NEEDING PEACE . . .

WEARY / UNHAPPY WITH YOUR APPEARANCE

Come to Me, all who are weary and heavy-laden, and I will give you rest.
—Matthew 11:28

1 Lying down here so easy.

2 Cheeks and breasts sag, but that's just what you see.

3 Flies hover in the air, invisible in the dark, greasy.

4 On the inside you flourish, thicker than flies on garbage.

5 The decay you experience as your joints creak and age is light as the branches of a poplar tree.

6 Lying down here gets easy

7 with the 3-D glasses in the *Sports Illustrated* 2000 swimsuit edition making you dizzy,

8 what you can't touch you can still see.

9 Flies hover in the air, invisible in the greasy dark,

10 and you lose weight by surgery alone, blitzkrieg knife leaving you wounded and drowsy.

11 A voice gubbles to you about people who don't exist except in a script. Your jawbone long as the arm of a giant crane, and your skin green.

12 Lying down here

13 every day everything sleazy

14 makes beauty possible.

15 Flies helicopter over your stink, hard to see in the dark, greasy with oil.

16 Your face all eyes, impossibly easy.

17 Vision makes vertigo,

18 makes lying down here simple.

19 Flies in the air, massing unseen.

WORRIED

For this reason I say to you, do not be worried about your life, as to what you will eat or what you will drink; nor for your body, as to what you will put on. Is not life more than food, and the body more than clothing?

—Matthew 6:25

1 Could you add a single hour to your life by worrying?

2 You could be a vegetarian, or stop driving in cars.

3 *Be anxious for nothing*, but save yourself one more hour to hold up your head from the pillow above the IV drip where the TV hangs from the ceiling.

4 The ice cream melts on your emperor's tongue, silting taste buds in the darkness of your upper mouth.

5 The clothing feels good too, but there is too much of it and every day is not enough.

6 *Is not life more than food, and the body more than clothing?*

7 And why are you worried about clothing?

8 The crows and grackles on your street are not worrying.

9 They have no combines with flat screen monitors, and to their children they say enough is enough.

10 Look for something we'll tentatively call righteousness and you'll get the cars.

11 Try to control your mouth.

12 Sounds of longing for plasma screens should not echo off the ceiling.

13 Your mouth too has a ceiling;

14 its words are clothing

15 for your mouth.

16 Tomorrow will have its own words. For none of them should you be worrying.

17 The peace which you experience only in air-conditioned luxury cars

18 passing cheaper cars and it's enough.

19 Enough is never enough.

20 There are books stacked to the ceiling.

21 They are objects like cars

22 or clothing.

23 Stop worrying.

24 The mountain's ragged mouth

25 slips under the sea's heart. The sea's mouth

26 indistinguishable from God's booming enough

27 worrying, I say. There shall be no end of worrying.

28 Don't think then that there is some arbitrary expense ceiling,

29 or say to yourself, "What will we wear for clothing

30 or do for cars?"

31 *He burns the chariots with fire… he cuts the spear in two.* But these are already hybrid cars.

32 On Page Six the wireless mike like a snake in front of her mouth,

33 and Britney Spears has rubbed fried chicken grease on a $6,700 Zac Posen gown.

34 *OK!* magazine's million dollars was not enough.

35 As you stare at the TV on the ceiling

36 you think Could I add a single hour to my life by worrying?

37 And cars will never be enough.

38 Mouth these words to the ambulance ceiling:

39 your clothes do not match your worrying.

WANTING TO BE A CHRISTIAN

Woe to you, scribes and Pharisees, hypocrites! For you build the tombs of the prophets and adorn the monuments of the righteous…. You serpents, you offspring of vipers, how will you escape the judgment of hell?

—Matthew 23:29, 33

1 The priest reads the Bible and is silent.

2 Even vipers have kids and it is sad to see, sadder to admit

3 him standing there closer than a Pharisee.

4 Robin flies into my window, leaves no dent,

5 is silent.

6 The jailer wakes up after an earthquake, he

7 wants to be a Christian, to be free

8 as the injured robin heaven-bent

9 and silent,

10 for the cat stalks and the bird walks

11 slowly from its encounter with transparency,

12 my window glass not a temple curtain rent

13 symbolically, not even bent

14 bars freed Paul and Silas—and me,

15 I read like a cat, quietly.

NEEDING PEACE

[for the 108 Afghan civilians killed by NATO air strikes in July 2007, and the six Canadian soldiers killed by a roadside bomb the same week]

1 In Afghanistan the poppies grow,

2 beside roadside bombs, row on row—

3 and six bodies stack for home

4 and vultures, casting shadows, fly

5 above the trail where sappers go.

6 Who are the dead? Last week we knew

7 about a half a dozen or so,

8 but we need our weapons from the sky

9 in Afghanistan.

10 Some Afghan bodies on their backs and in a row,

11 headless and rotting from the sun's harsh glow,

12 the same position the addicts lie

13 in Canada, where through the sky

14 we hear the jets descend so low

15 from Afghanistan.

You Have Left Home

1 Jesus slept.

2 When they woke him he uttered no threats to the wind; he thought of his absent parents, the DNA evidence that might have proven his lineage, the technology of rising from the dead. And Jesus wept.

3 Jesus felt threatened by technology that did not yet exist. Perhaps this was a function of narrative technique.

4 But he knew how to be powerless and dead.

5 He knew how to keep talking to the sea.

6 He knew that people wanted to eat his human flesh.

7 He dreamed of black rats running in the street after rain.

SOURCES

Most of the poem titles are from the section called "Where To Find Help When" in *The New Testament with Psalms and Proverbs,* Gideons International in Canada, 2004 edition. Biblical quotations are also from this edition.

Information about Ludwig Wittgenstein is largely from Ray Monk's 1990 biography *Ludwig Wittgenstein: The Duty of Genius.* Wittgenstein quotations come from *Philosophical Investigations,* translated G.E.M. Anscombe, *Wittgenstein's Tractatus,* translated Daniel Kolak, and the Internet.

Parts of "Tempted to Commit Sexual Immorality" are freely adapted from Samuel Beckett's novels *Murphy* and *Watt.*

"Just Retired" owes something to John Ciardi's "Men marry what they need."

"Insulted or Intimidated" borrows a few words from Marilyn Bowering's "Widow's Winter."

All advertising slogans belong to their respective copyright holders.

ACKNOWLEDGEMENTS

I want to thank: Sharon Caseburg for helping me realize that this was a book, and for suggesting the visual form; Di Brandt, Lori Cayer, Clarise Foster, and Deborah Schnitzer for their useful comments; my editor Dennis Cooley for his attention to detail; Todd Besant behind the scenes at Turnstone; my wife Betsy Troutt for her unstinting support and encouragement; and the anonymous missionary who gave her a Gideon Bible in 2005, which then became mine. Thanks as well to the Manitoba Arts Council for two grants that helped buy me time.

Some of these poems have appeared or will appear in the following publications, often in slightly altered versions: "In Danger or Threatened" in *The Fiddlehead*, "Advice on Being a Man" and "Advice on Being a Leader" in *Prairie Fire*, "Marriage," in *Arc*, "Failure Comes," "Contemplating Revenge," and "Contemplating Revenge (once more)" in *Dandelion*, "Unemployed/ Tempted to Abuse Credit" in *Contemporary Verse 2*, "Tempted to Steal/ Receiving Spam" in the anthology *A/Cross Sections: New Manitoba Writing* (2007), "Alone" in *The Malahat Review*. My appreciation to all the editors involved.

HELPFUL SCRIPTURE PASSAGES

ADVICE ON BEING A LEADER
1 Thessalonians 4:3–5

ADVICE ON BEING A MAN
Ephesians 6:2, Colossians 3:20

ADVICE ON BEING A PRO ATHLETE
Romans 13:13–14; 1 Corinthians 3:16–17

AFRAID
Mark 4:35–41, Psalm 56:3–4, 10–11, Isaiah 41:10

ALONE
Psalm 42: 5–11

BEREAVED / BROKENHEARTED
1 Thessalonians 4:13–18; Revelation 21:3–5; Psalm 147:3

BITTER OR CRITICAL
Matthew 7:1–5; Romans 14:10–13; 1 Corinthians 4:5; Psalm 73:21–25

CONSCIOUS OF SIN
Luke 15:11–24; 1 John 1:5–10; Psalm 51, 103:12

CONTEMPLATING REVENGE
Romans 12:17–19; 1 Thessalonians 5:15; 1 Peter 2:21–23

DEATH
Sister Anne Catherine Emmerich, Mel Gibson

DESPERATE (AT YOUR WITS' END)
Psalm 55:16, 17, 22; 61:1–3, 94:18–19, 22; 121:1–2, 7, 8

DISTRESSED OR TROUBLED
Romans 8:28–39; 2 Corinthians 4:8, 9, 16–18; Psalm 9:9, 10, 50:14–15

DIVORCE
Mark 10:1–12; Romans 7:2–3; Psalm 86:1, 7

DOUBT
Mark 8:23; John 20:24–29; Psalm 53:1

DRINK ABUSE
1 Corinthians 10:31; Ephesians 5:18; 1 Thessalonians 5:6–8

DRUG ABUSE
John 8:34–36; Psalm 139:1–5, 13, 14;
1 Corinthians 6:12, 19–20

FAILURE COMES
Hebrews 4:14–16; Psalm 73:26;
Psalm 77; Psalm 84:11

FAITH IS WEAK
Matthew 6:25; 8:5–13; Genesis 5–9;
Luke 12:22–31; Hebrews 11

FEAR
John 3:16; John 14:1–3; Revelation
21:4; Psalm 23:4

FRIENDS FAIL
Luke 17:3, 4; 2 Timothy 4:16–18;
Psalm 27:10–14; Psalm 41

ILL OR IN PAIN
2 Corinthians 12:9, 10; James 5:14–16;
Psalm 38:3–10, 69:29, 30, 103:1–4

IN DANGER OR THREATENED
Mark 4:37–41; 1 Peter 3:13, 14;
Psalm 27:1–3, 118:6–9

INADEQUACY
1 Corinthians 1:25–31; Philippians
4:12, 13, 138:8

INSULTED OR INTIMIDATED
1 Peter 2:20–23; Psalm 3, 55:20–22

JUST RETIRED
Matthew 6:33, 34; Philippians 4:12,
13

LONELY
1 Corinthians 7:1–9, 32–38;
Revelation 3:20

LOOKING FOR A JOB/ MADE REDUNDANT
Colossians 3:17, 23; Psalm 71:3

MARRIAGE
Matthew 19:4–6; Ephesians 5:22–23;
Hebrews 13:4

PRAYING / READING GRAFFITI
Luke 11:1–13; John 14:12–14; James
5:13, 16; 1 John 5:14, 15; Psalm
66:17, 20

SLEEPLESS
Matthew 11:28; Psalm 3; Psalm 4:8

SEXUAL IMMORALITY
1 Corinthians 6:9, 10, 13; Galatians
5:19–23; 1 Thessalonians 4:3–7

TEMPTED TO COMMIT SUICIDE
1 Corinthians 3:16–17; Psalm
42:5–11, 139:1–5, 13–14

TEMPTED TO LIE
John 8:44; Ephesians 4:25; Revelation
21:8

TEMPTED TO STEAL / RECEIVING SPAM
Romans 13:9, 10; Ephesians 4:28;
Hebrews 13:5

IN DANGER OR THREATENED
Mark 4:37–41; 1 Peter 3:13–14;
Psalm 27:1–3, 118:6–9

DISTRESSED OR TROUBLED
Romans 8:28–39; 2 Corinthians
4:8, 9, 16–18; Psalm 9:9; Psalm 10,
50:14–15

THANKFULNESS
2 Corinthians 2:14; Ephesians
5:18–20; Psalm 92:1–5; Psalm 100

UNEMPLOYED / TEMPTED TO ABUSE
CREDIT
Philippians 4:11–13; Psalm 37:7, 25

VICTIMIZED
Hebrews 13:6; Psalm 37:8–11, 34;
Psalm 59:3–4, 9, 10

WANTING TO BE A CHRISTIAN
Acts 16:10–40; John 1:12, 3:14–18;
Matthew 23:29, 33

WEARY / UNHAPPY WITH YOUR
APPEARANCE
Matthew 11:28–30; 2 Corinthians
4:16–18; Galatians 6:9

WORRIED
Matthew 6:25–34; Philippians 4:6–7;
Psalm 46

YOU HAVE LEFT HOME
Mark 10:28–30; Psalm 121; Luke
15:11–32

WHERE TO FIND HELP WHEN ...